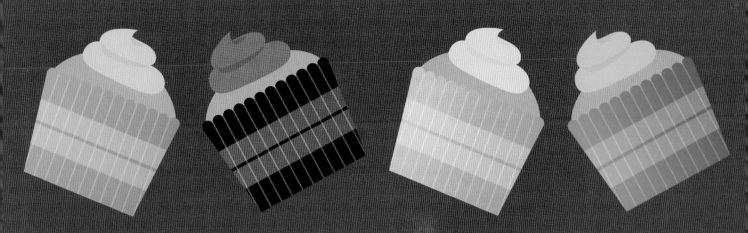

Hobby Time!

BAKING

KATIE MARSHALL

PowerKiDS
press

CONTENTS

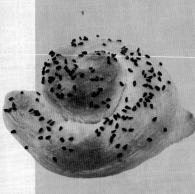

GETTING STARTED

Whether it's cupcakes, brownies, or bread, there's nothing more exciting than sharing a homemade snack. And after the hard work of baking, you definitely deserve a treat!

Baking is easy as pie (and just as tasty) once you know how. This book carefully explains the main baking techniques, then gives you step-by-step instructions to complete 10 delicious recipes. Each one will help you master different skills.

Dairy-free

Egg-free

Gluten-free

There are **gluten**-, **dairy**-, and egg-free options included. We've made these recipes easy to spot with special symbols. (Some people can't eat certain ingredients, so you should always check for any allergies before offering your goodies.)

Before you begin each recipe, remember to wash your hands and put on an apron. Read all the instructions through first, so you'll know exactly what you need to do. Once that's done, carefully measure out all your ingredients. Then you'll be ready to bake!

ESSENTIAL EQUIPMENT

There are a few things you should have in your kitchen to make sure you're ready to bake.

APRON Wear this to keep your clothes from getting dirty!

SPOONS Use big plastic or wooden spoons for mixing ingredients. Measuring spoons help you to prepare small amounts of ingredients.

MEASURING CUP A cup with measurements on it so you can tell how much liquid is inside.

BOWLS It's useful to have bowls in a few different sizes. They can hold your ingredients, or you can use them to mix ingredients together.

KITCHEN SCALES It's important to check the weight of your ingredients so you can be sure you're using the right amounts.

SIEVE A wire mesh to get rid of lumps from powders or liquids.

BAKING PARCHMENT This special paper, sometimes known as greaseproof paper, stops baked goods from sticking to your trays and tins.

BAKING TRAYS AND TINS These metal containers help baked goods cook by **conducting** an oven's heat, and also help baked goods keep their shape.

OVEN GLOVES These are a must whenever you're getting things out of the oven. They protect your hands from hot trays and tins.

TIMER Use one of these to make sure your baked goods will be cooked perfectly.

A NOTE ABOUT MEASUREMENTS

Measurements are given in U.S. form with metric in parentheses. The metric conversion is rounded to make it easier to measure.

WIRE RACK It's important to cool some baked goods out of the tins they were cooked in so they don't go soggy.

PASTRY OR COOKIE CUTTERS Cut pastry or dough into fun shapes!

BAKING TECHNIQUES

Baking involves some key skills. Here are the most important ones:

GREASING It's important to put a small amount of oil or butter on the inside of a baking pan with a brush or some kitchen paper towel. This stops your baked goods from sticking to the pan.

SIFTING Putting flour or other dry ingredients through a sieve gets rid of lumps, and gets air into your baked goods to help them rise.

CREAMING The back of a wooden spoon is just right for smoothly blending butter and sugar together against the side of a bowl.

RUBBING IN Rub flour and a fat, like butter, between your fingertips. The mixture will look just like breadcrumbs when you're finished.

MIXING The easiest way to combine ingredients is to stir them together in a bowl using a spoon.

ROLLING To flatten out dough or pastry, sprinkle some flour onto a flat surface, then place your dough on top. Roll a rolling pin over the dough in every direction to flatten it.

TESTING IF A CAKE OR BREAD IS READY

It's important not to open the oven door when you're baking, as it might stop things from rising. Each recipe will give you a range of cooking time, such as "20–25 minutes." When your cake or bread has cooked for the minimum amount of time, it's safe to open the oven to test it.

CAKE Put a **skewer** into the center of the cake. If it comes out clean, the cake is ready. If not, bake for five more minutes, then check again.

BREAD The bread should look golden. Carefully lift it up with a paper towel and tap the bottom. It will sound hollow if it is completely cooked.

KNEADING This process involves stretching and folding dough with the heels of your hands. It spreads an ingredient called **yeast** through the dough and wakes up something called gluten, which gives many baked goods their structure.

SIMPLE CUPCAKES

These yummy cupcakes are both super easy to make and a good way to master the basics of baking. Get a wooden spoon out and you'll be ready to mix!

Makes 12 cupcakes

STEP 1

Preheat your oven to 350°F (180°C). Put 12 baking cups into the holes of a muffin tray.

STEP 2

Cream the butter and sugar in a large bowl using a wooden spoon.

STEP 3

Combine the eggs and vanilla extract in a small bowl. Add them to the butter and sugar, then mix it all together.

YOU WILL NEED

4½ ounces (130 g) superfine sugar

2 large eggs

4½ ounces (130 g) soft, unsalted butter

4½ ounces (130 g) **self-rising** flour

1 tsp vanilla extract

2 tbsp milk

STEP 4

Sift the flour into the mixture, then add the milk. Combine it all with your spoon.

STEP 5

Carefully spoon the mixture into the 12 cups.

STEP 6

Bake for 18–20 minutes. Cool for 10 minutes in the tray, then carefully move the cupcakes to a cooling rack. Decorate with your choice of icing.

Turn to pages 28-29 for icing recipes and decoration tips!

ZESTY TWIST

Add a lemony kick to your cakes by replacing the milk and vanilla extract with the zest of a lemon and 2 tbsp of lemon juice.

SHORTBREAD

You only need three ingredients for these buttery shortbread cookies—and you can make them into any shape you want!

Makes 8–10 cookies

 EGG-FREE

YOU WILL NEED

2 ounces (65 g) superfine sugar, plus a little extra

4½ ounces (130 g) soft, unsalted butter

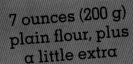

7 ounces (200 g) plain flour, plus a little extra

STEP 1
Preheat the oven to 350° F (180° C) and line a large baking sheet with baking parchment.

STEP 2
In a medium-sized bowl, use a wooden spoon to mix together the butter and sugar.

STEP 3
Sift the flour into the mixture and use the spoon to mix it into the sugar and butter (it might take a little while to get it all to stick together).

STEP 4

Sprinkle a little flour on a counter, then flatten the dough with a rolling pin until it is ¼ inch (1 cm) thick.

The flour stops your dough from sticking to the counter.

STEP 5

Cut out shortbread shapes using whichever cookie cutters you like.

STEP 6

Transfer the shapes onto your baking tray and sprinkle them with a little extra superfine sugar. Put the tray in the fridge for 20 minutes to make the butter harden, then bake for 15–20 minutes until slightly golden. Leave plain, or decorate with icing.

HANG 'EM UP

While they're still warm, carefully make a hole in the top of each shape. When they are cool, thread string through the holes and hang them up.

FRUIT SCONES

Mix up a batch of scones for a simple treat, then eat them with jam and a dollop of whipped cream.

Makes 6–8 scones

STEP 1

Preheat the oven to 425°F (220°C). Line a baking sheet with baking parchment. Sift the flour into a large bowl.

STEP 2

Add the butter to the flour and rub it together with your fingertips. Add the sugar, salt, and dried fruit.

STEP 3

Pour in the milk and stir with a spoon until it all sticks together.

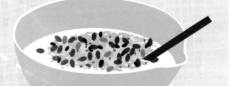

YOU WILL NEED

9 ounces (250 g) self-rising flour, plus a little extra

2/3 cup (50 ml) 2% milk, plus extra for brushing

1 ounce (30 g) superfine sugar

2½ ounces (70 g) mixed dried fruit

2 ounces (65 g) cold, unsalted butter, chopped into cubes

½ tsp salt

STEP 4

Put the dough on
a lightly floured
surface and flatten it
to make a disc that is
1 inch (2 cm) thick.

STEP 5

Cut out 6–8 circles using a
2½-inch (7 cm) pastry cutter.

STEP 6

Pop the scones onto your
baking sheet, spread
a little milk on the tops
(either with a pastry
brush or your finger) and
cook for 14–16 minutes.

Squeeze the
leftover dough
scraps together
and flatten again
to make the last
few scones.

EASY CHEESY

For a **savory** version,
leave out the sugar and dried
fruit. Add 3½ ounces
(100 g) of grated cheddar
cheese instead.

BANANA BREAD

This yummy loaf is a great way to use up ripe bananas that look past their best.

Makes 1 loaf

YOU WILL NEED

7 ounces (200 g) self-rising flour

6 ounces (180 g) soft, light brown sugar

7 ounces (200 g) soft, unsalted butter

1 tsp salt

3 medium eggs

1 tsp baking powder

2–3 very ripe bananas

1 tsp vanilla extract

STEP 1

Preheat the oven to 350°F (180°C). Grease the inside of a loaf pan and line it with baking parchment.

STEP 2

In a large bowl, cream together the butter and sugar.

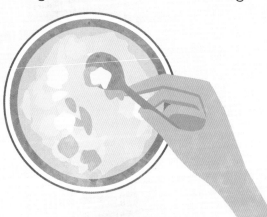

STEP 3

In a separate bowl, mash the peeled bananas with the back of a fork until they look like a **purée**.

STEP 4
Add the mashed banana, eggs, and vanilla extract to the sugar and butter, then stir together with a wooden spoon.

STEP 5
Sift the flour and baking powder into the bowl, add the salt, then mix it all together.

STEP 6
Spoon the mixture into your pan and bake between 55 minutes and 1 hour, until cooked.

CHOC CHIP SURPRISE
Add a little extra to your loaf by popping 3½ ounces (100 g) of chocolate chips in with the flour. Double yum!

GOOEY GRANOLA BARS

Granola bars are a great treat, whether you like them oaty or nutty!

Makes 16 bars

GLUTEN-FREE

YOU WILL NEED

(found in the international section of most grocey stores)

9 ounces (250 g) gluten-free oats

5 ounces (150 g) unsalted butter

5 ounces (150 g) soft, light brown sugar

2 ounces (50 g) golden syrup

STEP 1

Preheat the oven to 225°F (160°C) and grease an 8 x 8 square pan.

STEP 2

Put the sugar, butter, and golden syrup into a saucepan and carefully melt them on the stove over medium heat.

STEP 3

Remove your pan from the heat and add the oats. Stir together with a wooden spoon.

STEP 4

Pour the mixture into your pan and push down with the back of the spoon to make it all stick together.

STEP 5

Bake the mixture for 25–30 minutes until golden. Remove it from the oven and cut into 16 squares while it's still warm in the tin.

Cook the granola bars for 5 minutes more if you like them to be crisp!

STEP 6

When the granola bars are completely cool, cut the squares again and carefully remove to a plate.

GO NUTS

Use 7 ounces (200 g) of oats and add them to the pan with 1½ ounces (40 g) of shredded coconut and 2 ounces (60 g) of mixed chopped nuts.

PEANUT BUTTER COOKIES

These classic snacks are perfect for sharing with friends, and they only take five minutes to prepare!

Makes 24 cookies

YOU WILL NEED

1 medium egg

3½ ounces (100 g) soft, unsalted butter

2 ounces (50 g) granulated sugar

5 ounces (150 g) soft light brown sugar

½ tsp salt

¾ tsp baking soda

½ tsp baking powder

7 ounces (190 g) plain flour, plus a little extra

5 ounces (140 g) peanut butter

STEP 1

Preheat the oven to 350° F (180° C). Line a baking sheet with baking parchment.

STEP 2

In a large bowl, use a wooden spoon to mix the peanut butter and butter. Add both different types of sugar and mix together.

STEP 3

Add the egg, then sift in the plain flour, baking powder, baking soda, and salt. Stir it all until mixed together.

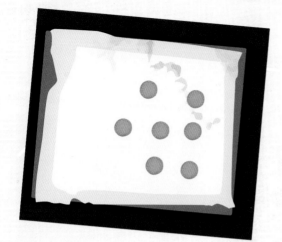

STEP 4
Shape half the mixture into
12 ping-pong-sized balls and
space out on your baking sheet.

STEP 5
Dip a fork in flour, then squash
each ball of cookie dough down,
making a crisscross on top.

STEP 6
Bake for 12–15 minutes until they
are golden but still quite soft. Cool
on the sheet for 5 minutes, then
carefully transfer to a wire rack.
Repeat with the rest of the dough.

JELLY THUMBPRINTS

Jazz up your cookies by making a
thumbprint over the crisscross before
they are baked. After cooking, when the
cookies have cooled
slightly, press the
thumb mark with
a teaspoon and fill
the dip with jelly.

CARROT CAKE

Carrot? In a cake? Sounds strange … but tastes great! Carrots keep the cake perfectly soft.

Makes 16 squares

 DAIRY-FREE

YOU WILL NEED

1/3 cup (80 ml) sunflower oil

5 ounces (150 g) soft, light brown sugar

2 medium eggs

6 ounces (180 g) carrots (about 2)

1 tsp baking soda

1 tsp baking powder

1 tsp cinnamon

1 pinch salt

1 ounce (25 g) plain flour

1 pinch ground ginger

STEP 1

Lightly grease an 8-inch pan and line it with baking parchment. Preheat the oven to 350°F (180°C).

STEP 2

In a large bowl, mix together the flour, sugar, baking powder, baking soda, cinnamon, ginger, and salt. Break up any sugar lumps with your fingertips.

STEP 3

Peel the skin from the carrots, then grate them and add them to the bowl.

STEP 4
In a cup, mix together the oil and eggs with a fork.

STEP 5
Add the oil and eggs to the bowl and mix well.

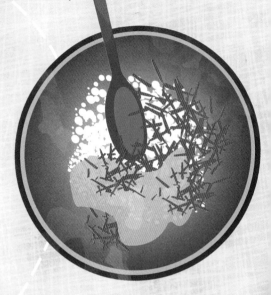

STEP 6
Pour the mixture into the pan and bake for 30–35 minutes, until cooked. Cut into squares and enjoy plain, or top with icing.

ONE FOR ME, ONE FOR YOU

If you want cupcakes instead, place 10 baking cups in a muffin tray and divide your mixture between them. Bake for 20–25 minutes.

SNAIL BREAD ROLLS

These rolls will teach you all you need to know about kneading—and they're shaped like little snails just for fun!

Makes 6 rolls

YOU WILL NEED

9 ounces (250 g) strong white bread flour, plus a little extra

1 tsp salt

1 tsp superfine sugar

⅔ cup (150 ml) warm water

¼ ounce (7 g) packet of fast-action yeast

1 egg, **beaten** with a fork

STEP 1

Preheat the oven to 425° F (220° C). Line a baking pan with baking parchment.

STEP 2

Put the flour, sugar, salt, and yeast in a large bowl and mix together. Make a dip in the center with a spoon.

STEP 3

Pour the water into the dip and combine the flour mixture with the water using a spoon.

STEP 4

Move the dough onto a lightly floured surface. Push it away from you with the heel of your left hand, then fold it back on itself. Push it away from you with your right hand, then fold it back. Repeat for 8–10 minutes until the dough is stretchy.

If your arms get tired, you might want to share the kneading with an adult!

STEP 5

Divide the dough into six pieces and roll each one into a long sausage. Coil the sausage round to make a snail shape, with its head poking out, and pinch the back end to make a little tail.

STEP 6

Place the snails on the baking tray and cover with plastic wrap that has been lightly brushed with oil on the bottom. Leave to rise somewhere warm for 30–45 minutes until the rolls have nearly doubled in size. Remove the plastic wrap, brush with beaten egg, and bake the rolls for 20–22 minutes.

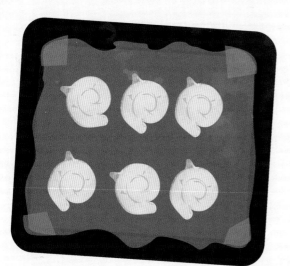

ADD SOME CRUNCH

Make your rolls more exciting by sprinkling their tops with poppy or sesame seeds before baking.

PIZZA TWISTS

Now that you've got your head around bread, it's time to have your own pizza party—with a twist!

Makes 8 twists

EGG-FREE

YOU WILL NEED

2 tbsp tomato purée

9 ounces (250 g) strong white bread flour, plus a little extra

1 tsp dried oregano

2/3 cup (150 ml) warm water

1 ounce (40 g) grated cheddar

1 tsp salt

1/4 ounce (7 g) packet of fast-action yeast

1 tsp superfine sugar

STEP 1
Preheat the oven to 425° F (220° C). Line a large baking sheet with baking parchment. Make a batch of basic dough by following pages 22–23 up to Step 4. Pop the dough in a bowl, cover it with oiled plastic wrap and leave it to rise somewhere warm for 30–35 minutes.

STEP 2
Sprinkle a little flour on a counter and carefully stretch the dough out until it is just smaller than a sheet of letter-sized paper.

STEP 3
Spread the tomato purée all over the dough to the edges.

STEP 4
Sprinkle most of the cheese and all of the oregano over the tomato.

STEP 5
Carefully cut the dough into 8 strips with a sharp knife.

STEP 6
Move the strips to the baking sheet and twist each one a few times. Sprinkle with the rest of the cheese and bake for 14–16 minutes.

MAKE IT GREEN
For a super–herby option, use green pesto instead of tomato purée and top it with crumbled feta instead of cheddar.

CHOCOLATE CAKE

This recipe is a piece of cake—tasty for a birthday party, or just for fun!

Makes 1 large cake

YOU WILL NEED

9 ounces (255 g) soft, light brown sugar

7 ounces (200 g) self-rising flour

9 ounces (255 g) soft, unsalted butter

1 tsp salt

1 tsp baking powder

4 medium eggs

2½ fluid ounces (75 ml) milk

2 ounces (50 g) plain chocolate

2 ounces (50 g) cocoa powder

STEP 1

Preheat the oven to 350° F (180° C). Grease two 9-inch round cake pans and line their bases with baking parchment.

STEP 2

In a large bowl, use a wooden spoon to mix the butter and sugar together.

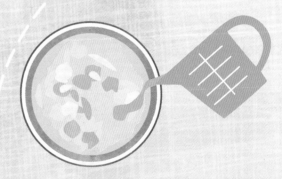

STEP 3

Beat the eggs in a measuring cup and pour them into the large bowl along with 1 tbsp of the flour. Mix well.

STEP 5

Sift the flour, cocoa, baking powder and salt into the large bowl, then stir in the melted chocolate and milk. Mix it all together.

Divide the mixture between both pans and smooth the tops. Bake for 20–25 minutes until firm to the touch.

STEP 4

Carefully melt the chocolate: ask an adult to help you to melt it either in the microwave or in a heatproof bowl over a pan of simmering water. Set it aside to cool slightly.

STEP 6

Leave the cakes in their pans for 10 minutes, then turn them out onto wire racks to cool completely. To decorate, make a double quantity of the chocolate icing on page 29. Spread one-third of the icing over the surface of one cake and put the second cake on top. Cover the sandwich cake with the rest of the icing and add candies on top.

MIX IT UP

Try covering the assembled cake with vanilla icing instead, and decorate the top with candies.

ICING AND DECORATING

Your cakes and cookies will be a treat on their own, but you can make your desserts special with icing and decorations.

BASIC VANILLA ICING

Enough for 12 cupcakes. Double the quantities to decorate the cake on pages 26–27.

In a large bowl, use a wooden spoon to beat 4 ounces (120 g) of soft butter. Sift in 5 ounces (150 g) of icing sugar and mix until combined. Then add another 5 ounces (150 g) of icing sugar, 2 tbsp of milk and 2 tsp of vanilla extract, and mix until smooth. Use a whisk near the end to make the icing even fluffier.

You can add a couple of drops of food coloring to your vanilla icing to make it more exciting.

CHOCOLATE ICING

Enough for 12 cupcakes. Double the quantities to decorate the cake on pages 26–27.

Follow the vanilla icing recipe, but when you add the second batch of icing sugar, only sift in 4 ounces (110 g). At the same time, add 1½ ounces (40 g) of cocoa powder.

Writing icing and colorful sprinkles, available in most grocery stores, are perfect for decorating cakes, brownies, and cookies. If you want to make something super special, why not add chocolate chips, sprinkles, Smarties, mini marshmallows, or even edible glitter!

You can make either icing dairy-free by using lactose-free milk, dairy-free spread instead of butter, and dairy-free cocoa powder.

ALLERGIES AND INTOLERANCES

Some people suffer from allergies that make their bodies react badly to certain types of food—even a small trace can make them extremely ill. Other people might not be allergic, but may have an intolerance. That means they have difficulty digesting certain types of food, but their reaction is not as severe as that of an allergy.

Gluten, dairy, eggs, and nuts are the main substances in this book that people might be allergic to. When baking for friends and family, check for any allergies before you start cooking. We've highlighted recipes that avoid certain food types, but it's often possible to swap tricky ingredients for special ones that are allergen-free.

Nowadays, there are lots of dairy-free alternatives, such as soy milk, almond milk, and vegetable-oil spreads (to use instead of butter). Some of these will add a slightly different flavor to your baking, and might affect the look or texture, but should make a dairy recipe suitable for someone who is allergic.

Eggs do lots of important things in baking. It might be safer to stick to egg-free breads if you have guests with egg allergies, but if you really want to try a recipe that includes eggs, look on the internet to find out about egg substitutes.

Gluten plays an important part in some baked goods, so it's not always possible to have a gluten-free option. You can replace self-rising flour with gluten-free self-rising flour, but the results may vary. You can also buy gluten-free baking powder.

GLOSSARY

ALLERGEN Something that can cause somebody to have an allergic reaction.

BAKING SODA A white powder that reacts with other ingredients in baking to make things rise.

BEAT To mix or stir ingredients together until they're combined.

CONDUCT To transfer heat.

DAIRY Describes something made from cow's milk.

FOOD COLORING A liquid or gel that can add extra or unusual color to food.

GLUTEN A protein found in wheat and other grains. It allows dough to stretch.

GRANULATED Describes little crystals of sugar.

LACTOSE-FREE Describes products that don't contain dairy.

PURÉE Cooked food that has been blended.

SAVORY Food that isn't sweet, such as bread.

SELF-RISING FLOUR A type of flour that has special ingredients to help baked goods rise.

SKEWER A long piece of metal or wood with a sharp point, used in cooking.

WHISK A stirring tool designed to get air into a mixture.

YEAST An ingredient used to make bread rise.

ZEST The skin of citrus fruits—it has a strong flavor.

USEFUL WEBSITES

PowerKids Press has developed an online list of websites related to the subject of this book. This site is updated regularly. Please use this link to access the list:

www.powerkidslinks.com/ht/bake

INDEX

Published in 2018 by **The Rosen Publishing Group, Inc.**
29 East 21st Street, New York, NY 10010

Cataloging-in-Publication Data
Names: Marshall, Katie.
Title: Baking / Katie Marshall.
Description: New York : PowerKids Press, 2018. | Series: Hobby time! | Includes index.
Identifiers: ISBN 9781499434293 (pbk.) | ISBN 9781499434231 (library bound) | ISBN 9781499434118 (6 pack)
Subjects: LCSH: Baking--Juvenile literature.
Classification: LCC TX765.M37 2018 | DDC 641.81'5--dc23

Editor: Liza Miller
Designer: Simon Daley
Illustration: Ana Djordjevic
Photography: Simon Pask

Manufactured in China
CPSIA Compliance Information: Batch #BS17PK: For Further Information contact Rosen Publishing, New York, New York at 1-800-237-9932.